THE WEST COAST ROUTE TO SCOTLAND

The history and romance of the railway between Euston and Glasgow

BY GEOFFREY KICHENSIDE

DAVID & CHARLES

NEWTON ABBOT LONDON NORTH POMFRET (VT) VANCOUVER

To my parents,
who lived within sound of it,
used it,
tolerated it,
accidentally gave me my first
LMS timetable at the age of one,
and who put up with my frequent
photographic sorties on it for
more than 20 years!

ISBN 0 7153 7210 6

Library of Congress Catalog Card Number 76–20144

© David & Charles 1976

Photoset in 10 on 11 Times
and printed in Great Britain
by Redwood Burn Ltd Trowbridge & Esher
for David & Charles (Publishers) Limited
Brunel House Newton Abbot Devon

Published in the United States of America
by David & Charles Inc
North Pomfret Vermont 05053 USA

Published in Canada
by Douglas David & Charles Limited
1875 Welch Street North Vancouver BC

Introduction

The West Coast Route to Scotland . . . what memories are conjured up by this most famous of all railways in Britain, with a history stretching back as long as railways themselves. It includes two of the oldest sections of planned trunk main line (as distinct from short local lines) in the country – the London & Birmingham and Grand Junction – and its route includes what has often been claimed as the first mountain railway in the world, the climb over Shap Fell.

The Euston–Glasgow main line with its offshoots to Northampton, Birmingham, Manchester and Liverpool, is without doubt the most important trunk route on British Railways and uniquely has changed its character more than any other, for it has been virtually rebuilt completely from Euston right through to Glasgow as part of the vast electrification scheme carried out between the late 1950s and 1974. Indeed, the transformation can be seen not only in station reconstruction, track simplification and realignment, but also in the demolition of closed stations and other redundant structures, and in the rebuilding of most bridges along the route to obtain clearance for the overhead electrification catenary.

Apart from the branches from the Liverpool & Manchester Railway (L&M) to Warrington (1831) and Wigan (1832), the oldest part of the route is that between Warrington, in Lancashire, and Birmingham, opened as the Grand Junction Railway on 6 July 1837 to provide a link at Newton, from the L&M, to the south. Only a few days later on 20 July 1837 the first stage of the southern part of today's West Coast route was opened from Euston to Boxmoor (now Hemel Hempstead), and later stages completed the route of the London & Birmingham Railway by 20 September 1838. Thus before 1840 there was through rail connection from Euston to Preston via Rugby, Birmingham, Stafford, Crewe and Wigan. But the majority of today's West Coast route expresses to the north do not travel via Birmingham and instead use what is known as the Trent Valley line from Rugby via Nuneaton and Lichfield to Stafford, thus avoiding all the complications of the Birmingham area. The Trent Valley was a line born of the complicated railway politics of the 1840s and was eventually completed in 1847, by which time an amalgamation of the Grand Junction Railway (itself by then enlarged to include the L&M), the London & Birmingham Railway and the Manchester & Birmingham Railway had brought into being the London & North Western Railway in July 1846.

North of Preston, railway construction was not quite so far advanced and the going was not as easy, for the high ground between the Lake District mountains and the Pennines barred the way towards Carlisle, and the Southern Uplands in Scotland provided a formidable barrier northwards on to Glasgow and Edinburgh. Nevertheless the Lancaster & Carlisle Railway, incorporated in 1844, despite its inhospitable route over Shap Fell was remarkably completed in a little over two years and saw its first train at the end of 1846. Yet this section was probably the most difficult to construct, for Joseph Locke, its engineer, had to carry the line from sea level around Hest Bank on the shores of Morecambe Bay to a summit of 916ft above sea level at Shap. The three miles or so between Hest Bank and Carnforth, where the line is within sight of the vast sands of Morecambe Bay forming part of Lancashire's Irish Sea coastline, have given the name the 'West Coast' route to the whole line, even though glimpses of the sea are but brief from a passing train.

North of the border, in Scotland, railway development, particularly in the Glasgow area, is almost as complicated as that in parts of England and certainly just as old. One section of line used today by Anglo-Scottish trains heading north for Perth and beyond, the Monkland and Kirkintilloch, in the outskirts of Glasgow, was opened in 1826, but it was another 22 years before the Caledonian Railway main line was completed between Carlisle and Glasgow. This section also included mountain climbing for it surmounted the Southern Uplands dividing the waters flowing south to the Solway Firth and north to the Clyde, north of Beattock, at 1016ft above sea level, before dropping down the Clyde Valley to Glasgow.

Thus it was early 1848 before today's through route between London and Glasgow was completed, and even then trains arrived in Glasgow on the north side of the city at Townend, for the line between Motherwell and Glasgow South Side was not finished until 1849 and the great Clyde bridge and Central station were not built until 1879.

DISTANCES

The varying ownerships of the railways when built or by later amalgamations have resulted in individual sets of mileposts being used so there is not a continuous sequence right through the 401¼ miles from London to Glasgow. The London & North Western Railway provided continuous mileposts from London to Golborne Junction between Warrington and Wigan, a new sequence starting from 0 was used between Golborne Junction and Preston, another from Preston to Lancaster and again from Lancaster to Carlisle, while the Caledonian Railway started again at 0 from Carlisle towards Glasgow and Edinburgh.

ARCHITECTURE

There is little doubt that some of the early railways spared no expense in building in the grand style. Some stations were superb examples of architectural splendour and, even on such everyday things as bridges, ornamentation in design or materials provided structures that really stood out. Moreover, they were long lasting, many surviving until recent times. But for the need to provide additional height for the clearances under overhead live wires, which brought the rebuilding of many overbridges, some of the original London & Birmingham bridges would have survived for many years more. Fortunately the handsome tunnel entrances, for example, those at Watford and Kilsby, are still now much as they were when built.

Of the stations there was nothing quite like Euston, with its imposing Doric portico, and the Great Hall which served as a waiting room for over 120 years. The magnificent panelled ceiling of the Great Hall was one of the largest in the world. The Great Hall was alongside the train shed, which was just that and no more, consisting of arrival and departure platforms, covered by a roof open at each end and on one side. In the extensions of later years this roof was widened and lengthened and survived until general rebuilding of the station took place in the 1960s.

The complete reconstruction of Euston station in the 1960s was long overdue, for its piecemeal enlargement over 50 years between 1840 and 1890 had added platforms in small groups, often tucked away at the ends of corridors or hidden behind offices. Indeed, it was doubtful whether many passengers in later years would have ever found platforms 8, 9 and 10 and it was just as well that few passenger trains ever used them, for they were mainly employed for parcels traffic. Today's modern Euston is without doubt a vast improvement for passengers and railway staff alike in its convenience, even though planning restrictions prevented full development of the station site with offices above as had originally been envisaged. Yet, it should have been possible to have embodied parts of the old station, particularly the Great Hall and the Doric Arch, the latter possibly moved to a new site in the new station, but they were victims of official vandalism by authorities who cared little for preserving the past.

TRAIN SERVICES

Looking back into the timetables of the last century, it is clear that even then the main line out of Euston was one of the busiest trunk routes in the country. Obviously it could not compare with the number of trains handled by some of the more intensively-used suburban lines around London, but dipping into the August 1887 timetable one finds a succession of trains in mid-morning, for example the 9.30 to Wolverhampton, 10.00 Scotch Express, 10.10 Liverpool and Manchester fast express, 10.15 stations to Bletchley, 10.30 North Wales and Lake District Express, 11.00 North Express, which included Edinburgh, Glasgow, Perth, Aberdeen and Inverness among its destinations. Once the initial excitement of through rail services had subsided there was little in the way of major improvements in facilities or speed for almost half a century. Coaches on West Coast route expresses by the end of the 1880s had six or eight wheels instead of four, but they were still basically of non-corridor compartment pattern, only a very small number had toilet facilities, and although by then one or two

Gateway to a station: the handsome lodges bounding the frontage of Euston station and which survive to this day, one of the few remaining relics of old Euston. On the cornerstones of both lodges are the names of places served by the London & North Western Railway, ranging from Wick to Tenby and Preston to Peterborough.

G M Kichenside

trains in other parts of the country had refreshment facilities on board they had not spread to the West Coast route. On Anglo-Scottish services trains halted at Preston for 25min while passengers dined in what must have been a quite unseemly scramble both to get served and to eat a four-course meal.

THE RACES

In 1887 the 10.00 Scotch Express from Euston arrived in Glasgow and Edinburgh at 7.45pm, a journey of 9¾hr. Further down the Euston road the rival 10.00 from Kings Cross to Edinburgh in contrast arrived at the Scottish capital by 7pm, still a journey of 9hr. At the end of July 1888 the London & North Western and Caledonian announced the acceleration from 1 August of the 10.00 train from Euston to reach Edinburgh in 8½hr, but on the very day of the new schedule the rival East Coast companies ran their 10.00 from Kings Cross to Edinburgh in 8hr. This was war! The West Coast then cut its schedule to 8hr and the East Coast replied with 7¾hr and finally timetables were abandoned altogether. The Edinburgh races lasted but a fortnight but in that fortnight the train crews of both routes showed what their locomotives could do in the way of fast running, and overall times had averaged just over 56mph between Euston and Edinburgh and 57mph between Kings Cross and Edinburgh. In the truce that followed it was agreed that standard times of 7¾hr should be observed by the East Coast route and 8hr by the West Coast.

But racing was not yet over, for in 1895 it broke out all over again, this time with London–Aberdeen traffic and in particular the overnight trains leaving Euston and Kings Cross at about 8pm. First one accelerated, then the other; half hours were cut, then more, and gradually minutes were pared off all the intermediate stages and again the timetable was eventually abandoned. This time racing lasted longer and was more fierce, but culminated in the remarkable time of 8hr 32min from Euston to Aberdeen on 21 August 1895, a time which has never been exceeded, for even on today's modern Inter-city services the fastest time between London and Aberdeen is 8hr 55min from Kings Cross. To be fair though the racing trains became lightweight-formation specials, with a duplicate train keeping to the regular timetable and serving intermediate stations. Nevertheless, the races had shown what could be done in the way of higher speeds and shorter schedules.

CORRIDORS, DINERS AND NAMED EXPRESSES

Another major improvement came in 1893 when the first train with through corridors and dining cars appeared on the West Coast route on the afternoon service between London and

The grand entrance to Hardwick's Euston in the 1840s.
This view was later blocked by the Euston Hotel.
British Railways

Scotland. Dining cars had appeared a year or two earlier but without through communication within the train, and passengers had to join and leave the car at intervening halts. As a result of the introduction of through corridors the afternoon Anglo-Scottish service acquired the nickname 'The Corridor' which persisted for many years afterwards, even to the second world war, by which time the train was officially known as 'The Midday Scot'. The other Anglo-Scottish day train, the 10am from Euston to Glasgow and Edinburgh, was given the official title 'The Royal Scot' in 1927 and with one of the overnight sleeping car trains, known as 'The Night Scot', formed the trio of Scot services which so characterised the West Coast route.

Not until the early 1930s was there any general speeding up of Anglo-Scottish services when the LMS and LNER agreed to abandon the standard times laid down after the 1888 races for the daytime services. This paved the way for accelerations culminating in the introduction by the LNER of a number of high speed streamlined services between Kings Cross and Newcastle and Kings Cross and Leeds, and in 1937 a new high speed service, known as the Coronation between Kings Cross and Edinburgh. The LMS replied with its Coronation Scot from Euston to Glasgow, worked by newly-built streamlined Stanier Pacifics, painted in a striking blue and silver livery. The Coronation Scot was booked to leave Euston at 1.30pm, call at Carlisle at 6.13pm and arrive in Glasgow at 8pm. It is interesting to compare the 4hr 43min from Euston to Carlisle with the 4hr 34min taken by the 1895 racing trains with much lighter loads but with much smaller locomotives. On the press demonstration run of the Coronation Scot in June 1937 the opportunity was taken to attempt to lift the British speed record which the LNER then held with 113mph. The LMS had nothing like the racing ground of the East Coast main line between Grantham and Peterborough, but on the outward trip between Stafford and Crewe accelerated over Whitmore summit to such an extent that it reached 114mph, little more than two miles from Crewe. Disaster was only a hairsbreadth away as it entered Crewe at 60mph but fortunately the train stayed on the track. On the return journey the demonstration run of the Coronation Scot achieved a time of 119min between Crewe and London, and while this was much shorter than the scheduled time adopted for the regular train it was the same as today's time for the electrically-hauled West Coast route expresses. Indeed it has been said that there is nothing that the electrics of today can do that has not been done already by steam, but it must be remembered that the best achievements by steam were on special occasions, usually with limited loads, an engine in

The entrance of modern Euston, less imposing but attractive in its own way.

British Railways

tip-top condition and almost hand-picked coal. The electrics of today can put up top-line performances reliably day-in, day-out, with no special preparation and with much heavier loads and often with more stops.

THE GLAMOUR OF A RAILWAY
The West Coast route has a romance and even fiction of its own, for it has been the setting for a number of novels and adventures, but the West Coast route has had some real life dramas, not least of which was the Great Train Robbery at Cheddington in 1963, when the southbound West Coast postal train was brought to a stop by a false red light displayed in an outlying signal and £2¼m worth of money was taken from mail bags. The West Coast postal itself, which is the principal mail train between London, Glasgow and Aberdeen, has a fascinating history of its own for it is one of the oldest mail trains in the country and for much of its life was one of those which picked up and set down mail bags while travelling at speed by lineside transfer apparatus and special equipment on coaches. At Euston while the 8.30pm down West Coast postal was standing at platform 2 being loaded up you could post a letter in the letterbox on the side of one of the coaches, provided you put the extra ½d stamp late fee duty in addition to the normal postage stamps. Your letter would then be sorted en route and if bound for an intermediate point might be dropped off at one of the mail transfer points ready for delivery early the following morning.

SPECIAL OCCASIONS
The West Coast route has always risen to its major occasions; in years past, for example, in the few days of August before the glorious 12th train after train would leave for the Scottish Highlands carrying parties ready for the shoot. There was the annual remove of the Sovereign and the royal household for the summer holidays at Balmoral which always entailed the running of the full royal train, usually leaving Euston in the early evening and travelling overnight to Ballater. In the other direction there was the annual exodus for Glasgow fair week, and further south Wakes Weeks and the pilgrimages in April or May to Wembley with dozens of trains on the Saturday taking supporters from northern teams for Cup Finals.

Today it is all so different. Gone are such titles as Scotch Express or Mid-day Scot; even the Royal Scot is little different from the other London–Glasgow expresses which run nearly every hour, with the fastest achieving a journey time of 5hr and most others less than 15min longer so that today you can comfortably leave London at 07.45, spend the afternoon in Glasgow and return by the last train of the day at 17.30 and still be back in London in time to get a train to one of the outer suburbs. Glaswegians can similarly spend an afternoon in London.

SIGNALLING

The major part of the modernisation of the West Coast route, apart from electrification, was in resignalling and other than in the 80 or so miles between Nuneaton and Weaver Junction, where several of the original signalboxes were adapted to control the new signalling, the rest of the route is under the control of only 10 power signalling centres. Colour-light signals are employed throughout, with continuous track circuiting, which means that trains not only directly control to danger the signals behind them, but also give an indication on the signal-box track diagram of their presence. What a contrast to 130 years ago when the policeman at each station signalled to trains by flags, and, since there was no communication between stations, trains proceeded at their peril on the time interval system!

The West Coast route is still the busiest trunk route in the country with six trains an hour scheduled to leave Euston through most hours of the working day arranged in groups leaving at about 5min intervals to make best use of track occupation and to leave space for slower freight and parcels services in the intervening period. With modern four-aspect colour-light signalling evenly spaced throughout all the way from London to Glasgow, clear headways of about 3min are often achieved between successive trains, each travelling at 100mph. This was a far cry from even recent times when seemingly the definition of block working on the LMS main line was not more than one train on the same line in one county at the same time! This might seem an exaggeration but in practice of three following expresses in steam days between Watford and London running at about 7 or 8min intervals, only one would be in the county of Middlesex at one time!

*   *   *

This album portrays the West Coast route in many of its moods over almost a century from the days when Webb compounds were the mainstay of motive power, through the later London & North Western period, the standard LMS and BR steam types, the diesels, which put up some brilliant performances in the 1960s, often in difficult conditions, to today's electrics. It is a tribute to the self-styled Premier Line, as the London & North Western was known, and to a line which can still claim to be the premier line of British Rail. It would indeed be interesting to hear the comments of Robert Stephenson, Richard Moon and Francis Webb who built and ran parts of this route on the transformation that has taken place on this oldest of trunk railway routes.

The route described

Route maps see pages 10–13
Chronology of the West Coast route see page 93
Gradient profiles see pages 94–5

EUSTON

Today's electric locomotives have so much power to draw upon that normally they make light work of gradients which in the past severely tested steam locomotives and their crews. Right from the platform end at Euston comes the one-time notorious Camden bank, steeply climbing at a ruling gradient of 1 in 70 for the first mile to cross over the top of the Regents Canal near Camden Town. For the first seven years of the London & Birmingham Railway from its opening in 1837 locomotives were not considered powerful enough to climb this incline and trains were hauled up by cable, powered by a steam winding engine situated near the top of the bank at Camden where steam locomotives were attached for the onward journey. From 1844 steam locomotives worked into Euston but from then until the end of steam in the 1960s most of the heavier trains out of Euston were banked by a second locomotive at the back of the train as far as Camden. Now, the electric Inter-city trains usually accelerate rapidly up the bank to achieve a speed of at least 50mph at the top when they enter Primrose Hill tunnel.

WILLESDEN–RUGBY

Speed is limited to about 80mph for the first five miles to Willesden but from here on trains can accelerate to the full line speed limit of 100mph. After passing the extensive freight marshalling yard and carriage servicing depot trains quickly reach Wembley, home of the stadium and the Cup Final; on the left just past the local station at South Kenton can be seen Harrow-on-the-Hill with its two spires, the taller one St Mary's parish church, and the lower one the Harrow School chapel. The modern building near the railway is a new hospital.

In climbing through the Chilterns between Watford and Tring up the valley of the River Gade there are a number of glimpses of the Grand Junction Canal (later the Grand Union), the route of which lies very near to the railway in several places between here and Rugby. As the train slackens speed slightly for the curve at Berkhamsted station the remains of Berkhamsted castle can be seen on the right of the line, and between Northchurch tunnel and Tring can be seen on the right the monument to the Third Duke of Bridgewater, father of the English canal system. The railway crosses the summit of the Chiltern ridge through a deep chalk cutting more than a mile long and emerges to drop gently down to the broad Ouse valley. As it leaves the cutting, prominent on the right is Ivinghoe Beacon, over 700ft high, and the lion cut out of the chalk, marking Whipsnade zoo.

After passing Bletchley and its little-used flyover built to carry freight to the south via Oxford and Reading, and the new city of Milton Keynes, the line passes Wolverton where speed used to be restricted for the curved deviation round the British Railways Carriage & Wagon Works. At one time the original main line went through the middle of the works area. The railway crosses the River Ouse by the handsome Wolverton viaduct and starts the climb to the higher ground of the Northamptonshire uplands where again the summit is breached by the long cutting at Roade. Here the slow lines part company with the main line and drop sharply away to the right to head for Northampton. Between Weedon and Welton the railway runs parallel not only with the Grand Junction Canal but also the M1 motorway, and in one place all three forms of transport lie side by side. Soon after veering away from the motorway at Welton the line passes through Kilsby tunnel, one of the major engineering works on this part of the route and which takes the railway through a major ridge of hills dividing rivers which flow east towards the North Sea and west into the Bristol Channel.

TRENT VALLEY

Once through Rugby, with its flying junctions north and south of the station, Liverpool, Manchester and Anglo-Scottish trains take the Trent Valley route through Nuneaton, Tamworth and Lichfield, avoiding Birmingham. At Colwich the Manchester via Stoke main line leaves the West Coast route; after passing through Shugborough tunnel West Coast trains slacken speed for Queensville curve at the approach to Stafford, where the original Grand Junction main line from Birmingham is joined. It is interesting to record that north of Shugborough there are no more tunnels on the West Coast main line to Glasgow until the very short one at Eglinton Street just outside Glasgow Central, a distance of about 270 miles, despite the climbs over the Cumbrian and southern Scottish mountains. From Stafford there is a gentle rise to a summit at Whitmore, after which the line drops to Crewe.

CREWE

Crewe is still a complex junction station by any standards, although the general decline in both passenger and freight, and cutbacks in train services, have lessened its importance in recent years. With nearly all lines through the station taking tortuous paths, with sharply curved approaches to platforms, speed is inevitably severely restricted. Crewe is still the

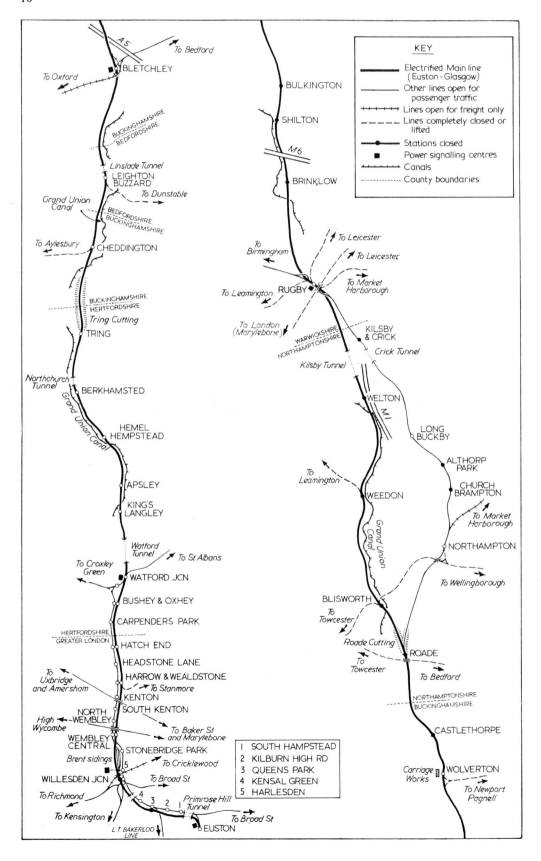

KEY

▬▬▬	Electrified Main line (Euston - Glasgow)
▬▬▬	Other lines open for passenger traffic
┼┼┼┼	Lines open for freight only
▬ ▬ ▬	Lines completely closed or lifted
●▬●	Stations closed
■	Power signalling centres
┼┼┼┼	Canals
⋯⋯⋯	County boundaries

1 SOUTH HAMPSTEAD
2 KILBURN HIGH RD
3 QUEENS PARK
4 KENSAL GREEN
5 HARLESDEN

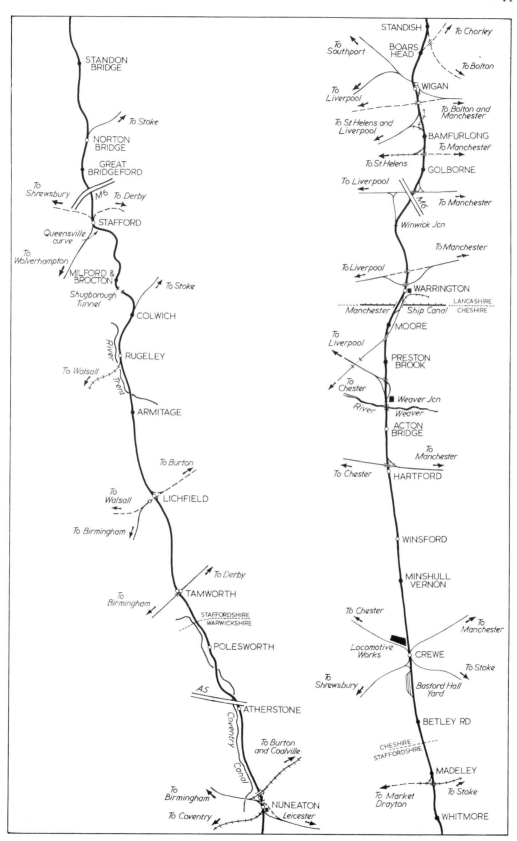

12

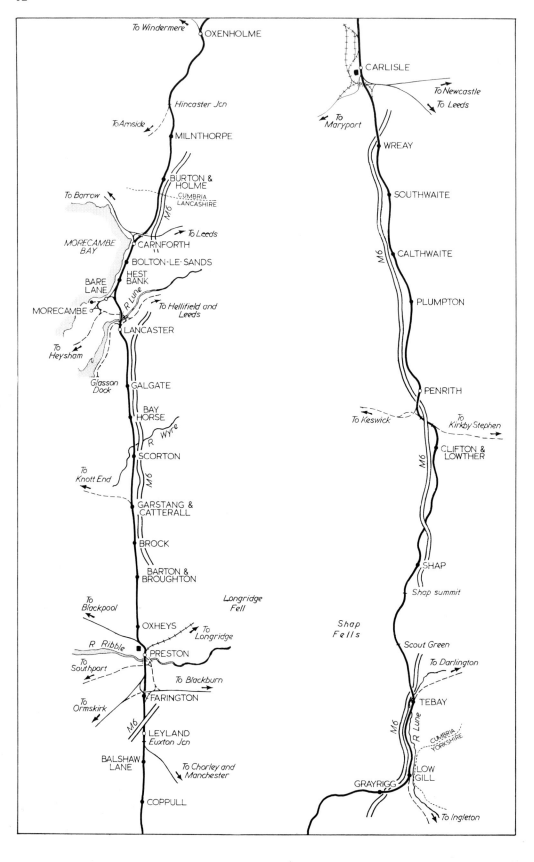

13

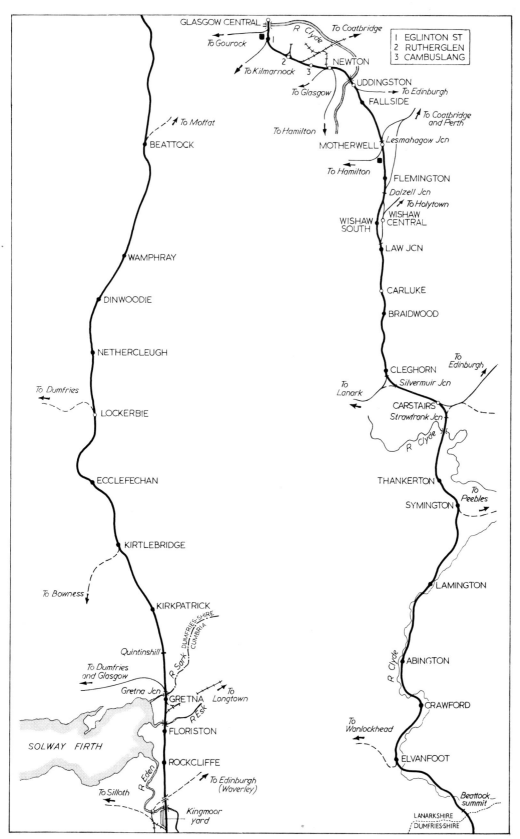

home of one of the great British locomotive building works, situated in the vee of the lines to the north and to North Wales. In recent years activity here has been confined to locomotive repairs rather than new construction.

ALONG THE WEST COAST

The West Coast route continues north from Crewe on the generally flat part of the Cheshire plain, crossing the River Weaver on Dutton Viaduct, and soon after losing the Liverpool line which forks away to the west. The up Liverpool line at Weaver Junction is carried over the West Coast route by a flyover. The West Coast route climbs steeply up and over the viaduct spanning the Manchester Ship Canal on the approaches to which can be seen the remains of the original route in this area before the canal was built. North of Warrington the West Coast route swings round the curves at Winwick Junction to pass under the original 1830 route of the Liverpool & Manchester main line, from which the Grand Junction was opened southwards to Birmingham in 1837. At Golborne Junction the Glasgow main line takes up the alignment of what was originally the Wigan branch from the Liverpool & Manchester, and threads the complex industrial and coalmining area of this part of Lancashire.

Wigan station was extensively rebuilt as part of West Coast route modernisation, but Preston, 15 miles further on, is still much the same as it was and entails a severe speed limit through the station until the divergence of the Blackpool line about $\frac{1}{2}$ mile north of the station. For the next 25 miles the line is virtually free from severe gradients, running more or less at sea level. Indeed, after passing Lancaster, where the castle on its hill overlooks the railway, the line runs along the shore of Morecambe Bay.

SHAP

From Carnforth the whole character of the line changes, gone is the industry of South Lancashire, and the flatter parts of the West Lancashire plain. Here the railway becomes a mountain line that starts climbing in earnest through Oxenholme, Grayrigg, through the Lune Gorge and Tebay, to Shap summit, 916ft above sea level, in only 30 miles from Carnforth. It is a land of wild, open moorland bounded on the west by the Cumbrian mountains and on the east by the bleak Pennines. Without doubt the best time to see this part of the route is on a showery April afternoon when black rolling clouds, sometimes full with hail and rain, propelled by a blustery nor-wester, starkly contrast with a strong sun and clarity of atmosphere behind to give a brilliance rarely seen in other conditions. Along this section the M6 motorway and railway are close companions, for the road builders followed much the same alignment as their railway forebears of the 1840s.

CARLISLE AND BEATTOCK

Carlisle, today, is still very much a border town, and although it has lost its railway character of 60 years ago, surprisingly several of its former services survive. The border with Scotland is not reached for another eight miles at Gretna but almost immediately climbing starts towards the Southern Uplands with, beyond the site of Beattock station, 10 miles of unbroken climb on a gradient of 1 in 77 to the summit at 1016ft. Again the line passes through bleak moorland before dropping down into the Clyde valley and the industrial area of the south east approaches to Glasgow with steel works, coalmines and factories.

GLASGOW

At Carstairs the line to Edinburgh makes a triangular junction with the West Coast main line while the continuation of the West Coast route northwards to Aberdeen and Inverness leaves the Glasgow route either at Law Junction or Motherwell. The Glasgow main line meanwhile threads the complex rail network of the south side suburban area, which carries a remarkably intense mixture of local electric, main line Inter-city and freight trains. More routes merge at the approach to the bridge over the River Clyde, and immediately on the north side tracks fan out into the platforms at Glasgow Central, the end of the line, right in the heart of the city centre.

Euston in the years before the first world war at 2pm with
the departure of 'The Corridor' to Glasgow and Edinburgh.
This train was so called because it was the first of the West
Coast main line expresses to be equipped with corridors
between coaches in 1893; it is seen here with the new
stock built specially for the service in 1909. The engine is
one of George Whale's *Prince of Wales* 4–6–0s.

Real Photographs

Below: Euston departure side platforms 12 and 13 in the
1950s.

G M Kichenside

Euston station was gradually enlarged over a period of 50 years around the Great Hall, and other offices including the shareholders' meeting room. The Great Hall had one of the finest panelled ceilings in the world, and was the finest waiting room of any British station. Although enquiry and seat reservation counters spoiled the Great Hall for many years in LMS days, British Railways cleared them away to other sites and restored the Great Hall to its former glory. At Christmas time the Great Hall was often the setting for carols sung by a choir drawn from railway staff when the acoustics were akin to those of a cathedral. *Left:* The statue of George Stephenson (which now graces the National Railway Museum at York) presides over a carol service in the late 1950s. *Above:* Official vandalism, with the demolition of the Great Hall and shareholders' meeting room in 1963.

Below: The Great Hall of new Euston. The rebuilt station is certainly more convenient for passengers than the old but planning restrictions prevented full use being made of the site to compare, for example, with Birmingham New Street station or the new station at Berne in Switzerland.

G M Kichenside, Kenneth Field, British Railways

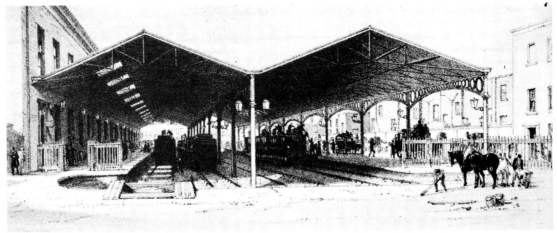

Old Euston changed little in its 125 years. *Above:* The arrival and departure platforms in the train shed of 1837. *Top:* That same train shed was later enlarged to form part of the arrival side and although modified in detail the general style of roof and ornamental supports were much the same in the late 1950s. This view shows platforms 3, 4 and 5. The latter was almost on the alignment of today's platform 5. *Left:* A detail of one of the gates of old Euston showing the London & Birmingham Railway coat of arms and the ornamental ironwork.

G M Kichenside (2)

Above: Coronation Pacific No 46239 *City of Chester* coasts into Euston platform 3 in May 1962. The lighter brickwork on the retaining wall behind the platform canopy marks the position of the bridge removed during the 1952 alterations.

G M Kichenside

Below: The hotel at the approach to Euston and which obscured the view of the Doric Arch behind it.

G M Kichenside

For Notes, see pages 410 and 411; for Continuation of Trains, see pages 408 to 411.

LONDON, RUGBY, BIRMINGHAM, WOLVERHAMPTON, STAFFORD, SHREWSBURY, CREWE, MANCHESTER, CHESTER, NORTH WALES, IRELAND, LIVERPOOL, WARRINGTON, PRESTON, CARLISLE, and SCOTLAND.—L. & N. W.

Out-door Goods Man., Southern Div., T. Shaw, Euston. Chief Mech. Eng., C. J. B. Cooke, Crewe. Asst. Eng., W. Dawson, Crewe. Min. Traff. Man., T. Mitchell, Euston.

Week Days—Continued.

Down.

Station																	
EUSTON .... dep.																	
Broad Street																	
Willesden Junction ...																	
Watford																	
King's Langley D ...																	

(Dense timetable columns, numbered 31 through 62 at foot.)

Station					
Shrewsbury 462					
Stafford .... dep.					
Great Bridgeford					
Norton Bridge					
Stoke .... arr.					
Macclesfield					
Crewe					

(Columns numbered 31 through 62.)

Cheap SATURDAY to MONDAY Tickets to LONDON from All L. & N. W. Stations.

Minimum fare
1st Class, 4/-
2nd Class, 3/-
3rd Class, 2/6.

. Tourists travelling to Stirling, Callander, Oban, Perth, Dundee, and Inverness can go via Edinburgh, breaking their journey at page xxii.

☞ For Through Services from L. B. & S. C., S. E. & C., and L. & S. W. Lines to Liverpool, Manchester, Birmingham, &c., see page xxiv.

"CITY to CITY EXPRESS."—London to Birmingham, leaves Broad Street 5 25 aft. (See column No. 71). Dining Cars, Typist, &c.

Euston, &c., to the North.] 406 [London and North Western Main Line.] L. & N. W.

Euston in the mid-1890s with Webb three-cylinder compound 2–2–2–2 No 2053 *Greater Britain* in the condition in which it was built in 1891 before the fitting of the square box cab extension seen on many LNW engines and often used as a splasher when driving wheels encroached into the cab space. In 1897 this engine was painted red as part of the celebrations for Queen Victoria's diamond jubilee for working the royal train between Euston and Crewe. Sister engine 2054 was painted white for the Crewe–Carlisle section and Caledonian engines for the stage northwards from Carlisle were blue anyway.

L&GRP

A section of the West Coast timetable taken from Bradshaw 1910 (a reprint of the complete book is available from David & Charles). The portion of the timetable portrayed makes an interesting comparison with other extracts in this book. Note the time of the 2pm from Euston arriving at Glasgow at 10.20pm. This is the famous afternoon service 'The Corridor', so called because it was the first Anglo-Scottish train to have corridors and restaurant cars.

Euston in the electrified 1970s. The line-up on 7 October 1971 shows a group of afternoon departures, including on the left, the 16.00 to Manchester, and centre, the 16.05 to Glasgow Central headed by Class 86 No E3163.

R F Roberts

The notorious one-mile Camden bank with its steep climb at 1 in 77 facing trains almost from the platform end at Euston. When the railway was built in 1837 locomotives did not venture south of Camden and trains ran down the incline by gravity and were hauled up by cable, powered by a stationary steam engine near the top. Here Jubilee Class 4–6–0 No 45642 *Boscawen* slowly climbs Camden bank with an empty sleeping car train for Willesden depot on 18 August 1962.

Gerald T Robinson

Today's electrics make light work of the climb up Camden bank and gone are the days when most trains needed banking assistance. An unidentified Class 85 electric locomotive accelerates towards Camden with a northbound express on 6 March 1973.

P A Dobson

English Electric Class 40 diesel No D224 *Lucania* leaves Kensal Green tunnel and approaches Willesden Junction with a down Liverpool express on 2 May 1964.

G M Kichenside

The disappearing face of Willesden Junction. *Above:* A June 1956 view with a Richmond-Broad Street electric train standing at the old High Level station spanning the main lines, with a Class 4 0–6–0 passing through on the down slow line on the left with an empty stock train for Willesden carriage sidings. Below is the same location taken from an almost identical viewpoint in February 1974. The High Level platforms on the Richmond-Broad Street line were rebuilt on a new site further away from the bridge across the main lines during 1956/7, but the main line station was closed and demolished as part of the electrification programme of the mid 1960s. One of today's empty stock trains from Euston to Willesden carriage depot is worked by electric locomotive No 86215. The bridge in the background has since been rebuilt.

G M Kichenside; John Goss

Left: Willesden Junction, even in the last years of steam occasionally offered a variety of types including through workings by Southern locomotives on South Coast–Midlands/North of England summer Saturday extras. Former LBSCR 4–4–2 No 32424 *Beachy Head* approaches Willesden in August 1956 with the Saturdays only through train from Hastings to Leicester.

G M Kichenside

Above: A West Coast Inter-city electric with air-conditioned stock passes Willesden on February 2, 1974 behind electric locomotive No 86024.

John Goss

A lightweight parcels train bound for Scotland headed by electric locomotive No 84004 passes the large carriage servicing depot between Willesden and Wembley on 31 May 1975.

Kevin Lane

SR West Country class Pacific No 34010 *Sidmouth* eases away from Wembley Central in 1959 with a through excursion from the Southern Region to Wembley for a sporting event. It worked the empty coaches to the goods yard at North Wembley, after which the engine ran light to Watford for servicing.

G M Kichenside

In the late 1950s a few of the LMS compound 4–4–0s returned to workings at the southern end of the West Coast main line into Euston, where for more than a decade their appearances had been very rare. They were largely used on outer suburban and semi-fast trains between Northampton and Euston; here No 41093 heads the 11 coach Saturday 3.05pm Euston–Northampton on 3 August 1957 near South Kenton. This was a regular Saturday duty during that summer but the compounds were often hard pressed with such loads.

G M Kichenside

Stanier 2–6–0 No 13270 heads a southbound freight on the up slow line between Kenton and South Kenton within a year or so of its construction. These engines were renumbered into the 2945 series in the mid 1930s. In the background is the bridge carrying the Metropolitan and Great Central lines over the LMS.

G H Soole

Three shots spanning more than 60 years, taken in the vicinity of the Metropolitan Railway overbridge at Kenton. *Top* is a September 1959 view of the afternoon Euston–Glasgow Caledonian express, headed by Coronation Pacific No 46234 *Duchess of Abercorn*. *Centre* is that same bridge but with only the double track Metropolitan line, before the Manchester, Sheffield, & Lincolnshire Railway built its London extension to Marylebone, which thus dates this photograph to before 1897. The locomotive is one of Webb's three cylinder compound Jeanie Deans 2–2–2–0s, the first of which were built in 1889. *Bottom* is the same area taken on 17 May 1913 after the New Lines, in the foreground, were added for suburban services but before electrification. This is the Sunny South Express from Eastbourne and Brighton to Manchester and Liverpool, including the SECR through coach from Margate at the front, headed by Jumbo 2–4–0 No 514 *Puck* and Webb four-cylinder compound 4–4–0 No 1926 *La France*.

Derek Cross; L&GRP (2)

About ½ mile north-west of Kenton was another footbridge used by many photographers. *Above:* Claughton class 4–6–0 No 5963 heads an up express in about 1926. *Below:* The same location on a Sunday in May 1962 with a Bletchley–Brighton excursion formed of diesel multiple-unit stock. The open space on the far side of the line had become formal recreation grounds by the 1930s.

L&GRP; G M Kichenside

The arrangement of tracks through Harrow & Wealdstone station changed on several occasions as new lines were added. When the original London & Birmingham double-track route was enlarged to four tracks throughout from Roade to Euston in the 1870s the additional lines through Harrow were laid on the west side to become the fast lines, while the original L&B tracks became the slow lines. When further widening was undertaken before the first world war for new suburban lines, at Harrow the additional tracks were built on the east side, the then existing slow and fast lines were slewed over and what had been the fast lines became the new suburban electric lines. *Above:* Jumbo 2–4–0 No 955 *Charles Dickens* heads the 4pm Euston–Manchester train through Harrow around the turn of the century. *Below:* Another Jumbo, No 2182 *Giraffe* built in 1875, passes Harrow with an up express around 1900. Today the third-rail dc electric lines at this point sweep round the outside of two carriage sidings.

D Weatherston collection; L&GRP

The West Coast route has unfortunately had its share of accidents, two of them the worst ever in Britain. At 8.19am on 8 October 1952 an up Perth–Euston express ran through signals in fog and ploughed into the back of a local train standing at the up fast line platform at Harrow. Seconds later, the 8.00am Euston–Liverpool/Manchester, double-headed by Jubilee 4–6–0 No 45637 *Windward Islands* and the unique Pacific No 46202 *Princess Anne*, which it was too late to stop, ran into the wreckage to form the mound of debris and twisted metal as high as the station footbridge. In the accident 112 people were killed.

Keystone Press

LMS Coronation Pacific No 46256 *Sir William A Stanier* on freight duty almost at the end of its life. It is seen passing Harrow on 15 June 1963, after the track layout alterations had been carried out here in readiness for electrification, but before the class was banned south of Crewe in 1964 because of insufficient clearance below the newly energised overhead electrification catenary.

G M Kichenside

The ill-fated LMS Pacific No 6202 was originally built as part of the Princess class but experimentally with steam turbine propulsion instead of cylinders. It was successful enough when running but spent more than half its life in shops for repairs and overhaul and was later rebuilt in 1952 as a conventional Princess class machine but with the slightly larger Coronation class cylinders, in which form it lasted but six weeks before being wrecked at Harrow. It is seen at Hatch End in its original condition on one of its regular duties, the down Merseyside express from Euston to Liverpool in the late 1930s.

C R L Coles

The LNW Royal train survived in its original livery until the second world war when it was repainted in LMS maroon. It is seen here passing Carpenders Park behind highly polished Royal Scot 4–6–0 No 6119 *Lancashire Fusilier* on 18 July 1934. The train was carrying King George V who earlier that day had formally opened the Mersey Tunnel.

C R L Coles

Occasionally photographers are lucky in photographing two moving trains together but here, near Headstone Lane on 2 July 1960, are three, with Class 5 4–6–0 No 45419 heading an up parcels train on the right, a Colne–Euston relief behind Patriot 4–6–0 No 45533 piloting Jubilee 4–6–0 No 45716, and on the left a Watford–Euston local electric.

J N Faulkner

Below: Class 86 electric locomotive No E3119 approaches the site of Bushey troughs in the early 1970s with a train of air-conditioned stock.

British Railways

About 60 years separate these two shots taken from the same location at Bushey troughs. *Above:* Problem class, also known as Lady of the Lake, 2–2–2 No 754 *Ethelred*, piloting a Webb Jubilee class compound 4–4–0, takes water on the last stage of the run into Euston. At this time many LNW expresses were double-headed since the Webb engines of the '80s and '90s were not up to the heavier loads by the turn of the century. *Left:* Royal Scot 4–6–0 No 46111 *Royal Fusilier* also takes a dip to top up its tender with an up express on 5 May 1962.

L&GRP; G M Kichenside

The short-lived streamlined crack express of the West Coast route, the Coronation Scot, introduced in 1937 to mark the coronation of King George VI and Queen Elizabeth, provided a 6½hr service on Mondays to Fridays between Euston and Glasgow but did little more than take traffic away from the Midday Scot which continued to run ½hr later from Euston, but only served Edinburgh. Here the down Coronation Scot in its striking blue and silver livery and headed by Pacific No 6221 *Queen Elizabeth* approaches Bushey. *Left:* Timetable advertisement for the Coronation Scot in the LMS winter 1939/40 timetable, which in the event because of the second world war, did not come into force and the Coronation Scot in common with many other expresses ceased to run from the outbreak of war.

L&GRP

Watford Junction has undergone many changes. Just before the first world war it was considerably enlarged by the construction of new terminal platforms to serve the inner suburban service between Watford, Euston and Broad Street running on the New Line. In the top view a push and pull train stands waiting to leave for Willesden, a service which operated until the New Line was electrified during and after the first world war. *Centre right* is Watford locomotive depot in August 1947; this shed provided power for local freight services and many of the outer suburban steam workings. *Bottom right:* Problems of electric working when power is cut off because of a failure or other incident; diesel locomotive No 25311 pilots electric locomotive 87009 on an up express from Watford to Euston on 25 January 1975 while repairs are carried out to the overhead catenary following a derailment at Bushey two days earlier.

L&GRP; R F Roberts; Kevin Lane

Experiment class 4–6–0 No 1553 *Faraday* approaches
Kings Langley station with a down express on 27 September 1913. Notice the remarkable bracket signal on the
left governing the down slow line, and the up slow/up
goods loop, with all arms having the characteristic LNWR
ringed ends denoting slow or relief line signals.

L&GRP

About a mile south of Kings Langley Jubilee Class
4–6–0 No 45586 *Mysore* approaches Watford Tunnel
in June 1959 with a Bletchley–Euston local.

Derek Cross

Block trains of single loads are common today but in the 1930s when the LMS built these special bogie hopper wagons block workings were uncommon. The hoppers were formed into complete sets which worked on regular duties between Toton yard and Wembley carrying coal for Stonebridge Park power station, a railway-owned power house which generated electricity for the Euston–Watford, Broad Street–South Acton electrified lines. Stanier 2–8–0 No 48363 heads north with the empty working near Bletchley in August 1964.

D A Anderson

Class 86 electric locomotive No 86222 leaves Linslade Tunnel between Leighton Buzzard and Bletchley with a down express in August 1974. The locomotive is fitted with the later type of crossed arm pantograph for current collection.

British Railways

Royal Scot 4–6–0 No 6104 *Scottish Borderer* heads up through Castlethorpe in the early 1930s. This station, together with Roade, was closed during the late 1950s and on the main line there is no station between Wolverton and Rugby, a distance of over 30 miles.

G H Soole

Between Weedon and Welton the West Coast main line, by now only double track, although the slow lines continue effectively via Northampton to Rugby, runs alongside the M1 motorway. At one point near here road, canal and rail are adjacent. Rebuilt Patriot 4–6–0 No 45534 *E Tootal Broadhurst* heads the down Welshman from Euston to Bangor in June 1960 alongside a very new and very empty M1.

Derek Cross

Although more powerful and reliable locomotives were built for the LNW in the first years of the present century, double-heading was not entirely eliminated and here George V class 4–4–0 No 984 *Carnarvon* and Claughton 4–6–0 No 1133 leave Rugby with an up Liverpool express in the 1920s.

L&GRP

An up freight headed by rebuilt Webb 0–8–0 No 1851 eases along the up main goods loop south of Rugby with a general freight in the 1920s.

L&GRP

Left: Claughton class 4–6–0 No 5979, newly resplendent in LMS crimson lake livery, heads the afternoon Euston–Glasgow/Edinburgh service through Tamworth in 1924. The train can be distinguished by the fine 12-wheeled elliptical roofed coaches built specially for this service in 1909, although existing clerestory roofed dining cars were also included in the formation.

L&GRP

Bottom left: Two Claughton 4–6–0s were not often seen together but here a pair head north with a down express through Shilton in the early 1920s.

L&GRP

Below: The Trent Valley Railway from Rugby to Stafford was opened in 1847 and ran through Tamworth and Lichfield, forming a useful by-pass to the Birmingham area for through traffic from London to the North of England. Somewhat sharper curves than on the London & Birmingham line, and coalmining subsidence, have limited maximum speeds, although today much of the route is passed for 90mph running and some stretches at 100mph. Here pioneer LMS diesel No 10000 heads through Lichfield with the 4.10pm Liverpool–Euston on 19 July 1952.

A N Yeates

An unnamed Claughton 4–6–0, No 98, approaches
Stafford on the up fast line from Crewe in the mid-1920s.
Stafford was not only the junction between the Trent Valley main line and the route to Birmingham but also the
cross-country line from Stafford to Wellington, whose signals can be seen above the tender, and also the isolated
outpost of the Great Northern coming in on the right from
Derby.

L&GRP

A general view of Stafford shed in 1925 with a variety of
LNW motive power.

L&GRP

An 1890s race up the West Coast main line between Crewe and Stafford with Lady of the Lake 2–2–2 No 134 *Owl* on the left with a mixed load on the up slow line, and a former Samson class 2–4–0 No 635 *Zamiel,* here seen in its rebuilt form as one of the 6ft Jumbos, with an up express on the fast line. The location is Whitmore troughs where both will take water.

F Moore Dutton collection

Taken only a few yards south of the photograph above, and on the other side of the line, Royal Scot 4–6–0 No 46140 *The King's Royal Rifle Corps* heads the up Mancunian over Whitmore troughs on 15 June 1957.

R W Hinton

Train spotters at Crewe take a close look at Greater Britain class Webb three-cylinder compound 2–2–2–2 No 2054 *Queen Empress*, in its remarkable white livery adopted for Queen Victoria's diamond jubilee celebrations in 1897. This engine was used on the middle stage of the royal journey to Scotland so that Her Majesty was hauled in order by red, white and blue locomotives. The livery was particularly complex and included apart from the base white, or more properly spilt milk, colour, lavender grey smokebox, chimney, and broad lining bands, dark blue frames and wheels, and blue and gold fine lining.

L&GRP

Royal Scot No 6138 *The London Irish Rifleman* coasts into Crewe with the up Royal Scot from Glasgow to Euston in the mid-1930s.

G H Soole

On the same track but about 40 years later electric locomotive No 86237 runs into Crewe with the 17.00 Manchester–Euston Pullman on 2 September 1974. Despite extensive resignalling at Crewe at various times, the track layout here has changed little.

Kevin Lane

Right:
To provide an accelerated service between Crewe and Glasgow to match standards south of Crewe with electric working between 1968 and 1974, pairs of Class 50 English Electric diesels were rostered to principal express passenger services for some of this period. Here Nos 423 and 445 leave Crewe for Glasgow on 7 April 1973.

G T Heavyside

Left: Mainstay of West Coast motive power between 1960 and 1967 in the interim period between the last years of steam traction and completion of electrification south of Crewe, was the English Electric Class 40, a massive design weighing over 130 tons and carried on two eight-wheeled bogies. Here No 307 stands at Crewe waiting to work a train for the North Wales coast line on 7 April 1973.

G T Heavyside

Left: Apart from its main line services Crewe was the hub of a number of local services radiating in all directions. Here Ivatt 2–6–2T No 41201, a design which appeared on the LMS just before nationalisation in 1947, waits to work a two-coach local to Wellington on 21 July 1962.
Right: The pioneer LMS diesel No 10000 for some of its life was allocated to a regular express freight working between Camden depot and Crewe. It is seen here after arrival at Crewe about to be uncoupled to go to depot in the early 1960s.

J E Bell; Kenneth Field

Left: A corner of the vast locomotive works at Crewe photographed in the 1950s. Crewe Works was originally opened in 1843 by the Grand Junction Railway to replace its original works at Edge Hill, Liverpool. From the works and the station came the town, which originally was administered by the railway.

L & GRP

Two comparative shots of Hartford station north of Crewe with, *above*, the last unrebuilt Royal Scot 4–6–0, No 46137 *The Prince of Wales' Volunteers (South Lancashire)*, photographed on a Liverpool–Birmingham train on 31 July 1953. *Below:* Another Liverpool–Birmingham train, this time in 1963 behind an electric locomotive.

R W Hinton; Kenneth Field

Stanier 2–8–0 No 48764 heads a coal train south-wards over the Manchester Ship Canal viaduct just south of Warrington on 1 April 1967.

M Turner

A 1950s shot of a northbound freight headed by an LNW 0–8–0 as it climbs towards the Manchester Ship Canal bridge near Warrington. The completion of the canal in the 1890s led to the building of the viaduct and the long approach embankments. The original course of the main line can be seen in the approach to the bricked-up tunnel mouth.

Kenneth Field

Stanier Pacific No 46220 *Coronation* heads an up Glasgow–Birmingham express near Springs Branch, Wigan, on 24 August 1961. On the left former LNW 0–8–0 No 49447 waits for signals with a local freight.
J E Bell

English Electric Class 40 diesel No 243 passes Springs Branch with a down block freight on 16 August 1971. Already track alterations and simplification are in progress ready for resignalling and electrification, completed in the following three years.
G T Heavyside

BR/Sulzer Class 25 No 7600 approaches the Leeds & Liverpool canal bridge, south of Wigan, with a down coal train on 17 August 1971.
G T Heavyside

Royal Scot Class 4–6–0 No 46138 *The London Irish Rifleman* speeds through Wigan North Western with a Carlisle–Euston express on 20 September 1958. The station here has been completely rebuilt as part of the electrification and modernisation programme.

R W Hinton

Wigan in the electric era with Class 85 locomotive No E3064 accelerating from Wigan North Western with the 09.00 Euston–Carlisle. The photograph was taken from the low level Wigan Wallgate station on 16 March 1974.

G T Heavyside

Boar's Head Junction, north of Wigan on the West Coast main line, seen *above* while it was still a junction in July 1939 with the line to Chorley and Blackburn diverging to the right, and *below* on 16 August 1971 after the station had been demolished and the Blackburn line closed. Brush Class 47 diesel No 1729 heads up the West Coast main line with a Glasgow—Euston express.

R F Roberts; G T Heavyside

Webb's Precedent class 2—4—0s with their 6ft 9in driving wheels, generally known as 'Jumbos', were hardly intended for freight work yet No 919 *Nasmyth* was so employed when caught by the photographer in the early 1920s on the multi-track section south of Preston.

L&GRP

Ramsbottom's Newton Class 2—4—0s, later rebuilt as Precedents, eventually formed a single class with several other types of LNW 2—4—0. All were extensively used for piloting on West Coast main line trains but by the 1920s large numbers had been withdrawn and the survivors of the 80 or so handed over by the LNW to the LMS at the grouping were used on secondary or branch services. No 1480 *Newton* works a return excursion from Blackpool in 1924, near Preston.

L&GRP

The section of the West Coast main line between Euxton Junction and Preston was administered by the London & North Western and Lancashire & Yorkshire railways who jointly leased the North Union Railway (originally the Wigan & Preston). It provided the L&Y with access from Manchester to Preston and Blackpool and thus carried not only West Coast main line trains but also heavy traffic from various parts of Lancashire to the coast. Here Lancashire & Yorkshire Railway Class 27 0–6–0 No 1125 heads a long rake of mostly six-wheel coaches on a Manchester–Blackpool excursion in the mid-1920s.

L&GRP

An unusual pairing was a Jumbo 2–4–0 and a Lancashire & Yorkshire 4–6–0, but Precedent class 2–4–0 No 883 *Phantom* is seen here piloting No 10456 on the afternoon Euston–Glasgow/Edinburgh service in 1924.

L&GRP

In the track rationalisation and re-routings undertaken as part of electrification a number of running junctions on the West Coast main line through Lancashire have been eliminated. The principal route from Manchester to the north now joins the West Coast main line a little way south of Preston at Farington Curve Junction where Class 40 diesel No 210 is seen with a Manchester–Blackpool train, while in the background a Class 47 diesel waits for signals with a down motorail train for Scotland on 31 July 1971.

G T Heavyside

The nearest that the West Coast main line gets to the sea is at Hest Bank between Lancaster and Carnforth, where the line runs along the edge of the mud flats of Morecambe Bay. LM electric locomotive No 86205 passes Hest Bank with the 09.10 Glasgow–Euston on 11 May 1974.

G T Heavyside

LMS Stanier Pacific No 6222 *Queen Mary* heads the 1.30pm Glasgow–Euston Coronation Scot at Oxenholme in the summer of 1939. Although this was the principal LMS luxury train the coaches for it were converted from ordinary vehicles. A new Coronation Scot train set painted in maroon and gold livery was built during 1939 but was shipped to America for exhibition at the New York world fair, where it was isolated by the outbreak of war in September 1939. Although the engine that went to America, No 6229 *Duchess of Hamilton* pretending to be No 6220 *Coronation,* having exchanged names and numbers, was shipped back during the war, the coaches remained in the USA as an officers' club for US servicemen and did not return to the LMS until the cessation of hostilities. The Coronation Scot never ran again and the coaches built specially, also the 1937 sets, were dispersed for ordinary service use and painted in normal livery.

L&GRP

The same location 26 years later on 15 May 1965, by which time diesels had taken over most services. English Electric Class 40 No D334 passes Oxenholme with the up Midday Scot, successor to the Corridor. In the intervening years many of the trees have been cut down.

Gerald T Robinson

Left: A spectacular view from the top of Grayrigg Pike through the Lune Gorge towards Tebay and Shap Fell in the late 1960s. A southbound freightliner train hauled by a Class 47 diesel coasts downhill towards Low Gill. Today the M6 motorway has carved out a broader trace to the left of the railway but generally follows much the same alignment.

John Goss

Bottom left: The completed M6 motorway overshadows the railway through the Lune Gorge scarring so much more of the hillside than the railway. Brush Class 47 No 1962 passes the site of the former Dillicar water troughs south of Tebay with a northbound passenger train on 11 August 1973.

G T Heavyside

Below: A little further south in the Lune Gorge English Electric diesel No D291 heads an up express from Perth to London on 28 May 1963. The overbridge here is the one prominent in the aerial picture on the left, on the lefthand extremity of the curve.

Derek Cross

Tebay.

Marshalling of Down Stock Trains.—Down Stock Trains for Carlisle, when in an unmarshalled state, must stop at Tebay for the purpose of remarshalling.

Trap Siding at north end of Yard.—The Trap Siding at the North end of the North Yard must not be used for shunting purposes.

Banking of Passenger Trains.—Down Passenger Trains requiring assistance from Tebay to Shap Summit may be assisted by a Bank Engine in the rear.

The Drivers of all Down Passenger Trains not timed to stop at Tebay, and requiring the assistance of a Bank Engine, must, on approaching Tebay No. 1 Box, give three distinct crows, and bring the Train to a stand with the Engine opposite the Indicating Post (painted red), erected on the Down side of the Line north of No. 2 Box. The Driver of the Bank Engine must sound his whistle as soon as he has joined the Train as the Signal to the Driver of the Train Engine to start.

Bank Engines.—No Goods, &c., Train which exceeds 19 Waggons and Break Van must be allowed to leave Tebay for the North without a Bank Engine.

Above: A general view of Tebay with a northbound ballast train headed by Class 5 4–6–0 No 44911 on 17 June 1967. The line diverging in the foreground is the former branch to Kirkby Stephen and Darlington; in the right background is the motive power depot housing the banking locomotives used for assisting passenger and freight trains up the steep climb to Shap summit.

John Goss

Left: A Britannia Pacific accelerates over Dillicar troughs with a southbound mail and parcels train on 5 August 1967.

John Goss

Bottom left: London & North Western appendix instructions for working at Tebay.

Below: Jubilee Class 4–6–0 No 45707 *Valiant* has drawn to a stand beyond Tebay station with a Blackpool–Glasgow excursion on 27 September 1961; the banker has come off shed and gently buffered up to the rear and after whistle signals have been exchanged the pair gradually get to grips and restart the train for the steep climb to Shap summit. Banking engines normally worked trains in this fashion uncoupled so they simply dropped off on reaching Shap summit without stopping the main train. It was however essential for the banking engine to keep pushing hard and not lag behind!

Derek Cross

Above: In the last years of steam working many of the now familiar types of block freight train were only just coming into operation. An unidentified Britannia Pacific runs downhill towards Tebay with a heavy load of steel pipes on 10 June 1967.

John Goss

Top left: Today's electrics take the steep climb to Shap summit in their stride more or less as though it was not there, except that during damp weather and, particularly, when working the slower moving freight trains, they sometimes have wheel slip problems. No 86232 speeds past Greenholme towards Shap summit with the 16.45 Euston–Glasgow on 11 May 1974. It is remarkable to think that passengers can leave London in the late afternoon and still see the beauties of Shap summit on a fine spring evening in daylight.

G T Heavyside

Bottom left: At the same location but 14 years earlier Clan class Pacific No 72003 *Clan Fraser* struggles towards the summit banked in the rear with a Liverpool–Glasgow express on 5 August 1960.

Derek Cross

Right: In the last years of steam, Mecca for many enthusiasts was the area around Scout Green signalbox, that lonely outpost in the wilds of Shap Fell, with very few levers controlling little more than home and distant signals in each direction and helping to divide the block section on the climb into shorter lengths. Now it has gone, replaced by modern colour-light signals supervised from Carlisle. Today's electrics now sweep by at speeds undreamed of in steam days and nobody spares a thought for the men who spent many hours in all weathers at this desolate spot.

Marion Canning

Above: In LNW days, indeed until the advent of the Royal Scot 4–6–0s in 1927, most Anglo-Scottish trains were double-headed on the part of the journey which included the climb to Shap summit, usually from their last stopping station travelling north so that often they would be double-headed right through from Crewe or Preston to Carlisle. This is the 1890s predecessor of what later became the Royal Scot service, the 10am Euston–Glasgow, climbing towards Shap behind Whitworth class 2–4–0 No 90 *Luck of Edenhall* piloting one of Webb's smaller 2–2–2–2s of the John Hick class, No 1536 *Hugh Myddleton*. By the end of the 1890s all Anglo-Scottish trains had corridors and dining cars but these features had not then long been in use, for dining cars had only appeared in 1891 and through corridors in 1893. Until then meals were taken at special stops, usually at Preston for Anglo-Scottish trains, where multi-course meals had to be served and eaten in as little as 20min in some cases.

L&GRP

Below: Right up to the end of steam in some instances the assisting engine was coupled ahead of the train engine for the climb to Shap summit, as here with Stanier Class 4 2–6–4T No 42439 piloting Class 5 4–6–0 No 44937 with a Blackpool–Glasgow train on 28 September 1964.

Derek Cross

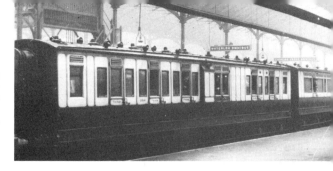

Eighty years of passenger coaches on the West Coast main line with, from top to bottom, early LNW corridor coaches of the late 1890s, LMS standard corridor stock of the 1930s and today's BR air-conditioned vehicles.

British Railways

Extracts from the LNWR appendix to the working time-table giving loads for single engines on the main line, together with banking of passenger trains over Shap.

The maximum tonnage for one Engine (L. & N. W) will be as follows :—
MAIN LINE.

Points between	Claughton.	Superheater.	Precursor or Experiment.	Renown.	6' 6'' and 6' S.L.
	Tons.	Tons.	Tons.	Tons.	Tons.
Euston and Liverpool, except American Specials					
N.B.—American Specials between London and Riverside must not be made up to more than 400 tons.					
Euston and Manchester (London Road) ...	440	420	350	260	200
Euston and Holyhead					
Euston, Carnforth, and Morecambe					
Euston and Crewe *via* Birmingham (both routes)					
Euston and Birmingham Expresses	440	420	300	225	170
Carnforth, Carlisle, and Windermere ...	400	350*	300	225	170

NOTES.—Through Trains not stopping intermediately between Crewe or Preston and Carlisle must in all cases take suitable Engine power from the last stopping place where assistance is available

On some sections of the Line where "Benbow" and "Jubilee" class of engines are working no load has been laid down, but this may be taken as being the same as the "Renown," and where no load is shown for an 18-in. Goods Engine this may be taken as 50 per cent. higher than a 6' 6'' Passenger Engine, and a 19 in. Goods as equivalent to an "Experiment" Engine.

Scenes at Shap summit over 75 years. *Top left:* An 1890s shot as a pair of 2–4–0s with the 12.40pm Carlisle–Euston express draw to a stand at Shap summit and the fireman of the leading engine climbs down ready to uncouple the pilot which will return to Carlisle. Notice the slotted post semaphore signal on the right. The train is formed mainly of non-gangwayed non-bogie radial eight-wheeled coaches, apart from the pair of six-wheelers at the front, one of which is a North British saloon.

L & GRP

Centre left: Just a week after the inauguration of full electric services between London and Glasgow No 86235 surmounts Shap summit with the 15.00 Euston–Glasgow on 11 May 1974.

G T Heavyside

Right: A Stanier Class 5 pilots a Britannia Pacific, with a 16-coach load typical of those often found in steam days, past Shap summit and starts the steep descent to Tebay, in 1964.

M Dunnett

Below: Interloper at Shap with WR Castle class 4–6–0 No 7029 *Clun Castle* storming up the last few yards of the climb with an enthusiast excursion to Carlisle on 14 October 1967.

J K Morton

The northern approach to Shap takes the West Coast main
line through attractive countryside near Thrimby Grange
where Stanier Class 5 4–6–0 No 45039 storms uphill
with an express freight on 31 August 1963.

Derek Cross

Shap station was situated a little below the summit on the north side and one of its features until closure was its attractive station gardens and hanging baskets. Coronation class Pacific No 46254 *City of Stoke on Trent* drifts down through Shap with the northbound Royal Scot in July 1962.

Derek Cross

The southbound Lakes Express, made up of portions from Keswick and other starting points in the Lake District, leaves Penrith on the first stage of its journey on the West Coast main line towards Oxenholme behind Stanier Class 4 2–6–4T No 42571. Ivatt Class 2 2–6–0 No 46431 waits on the Keswick branch with a lightweight freight. The date is 21 July 1962.

Derek Cross

Extract from the early afternoon page of the West Coast main line timetable from the September 1939 timetable. This service did not come into operation, for an emergency timetable replaced it on the outbreak of war, but it does nevertheless represent what would have been the peak winter service at the end of the 1930s. By this time the Coronation Scot at 1.30 from Euston was arriving at Glasgow by 8pm while the Midday Scot on Mondays to Fridays at 2.00pm from Euston ran to Edinburgh.

MAIN LINE "A"—LONDON (EUSTON) TO CREWE—WEEK DAYS —continued.

Table 60

Station		12|15	12|30		12|50	1| 5	1|15	1|30	1|30		1|30		1|55		1|35	1|45	1|55	2| 0	2| 0	2| 0		2| 7	2|25
LONDON (Euston)	dep.	12|15	12|30		12|50	1| 5	1|15	1|30	1|30		1|30		1|55		1|35	1|45	1|55	2| 0	2| 0	2| 0		2| 7	2|25
Willesden Junction	"	12|23											1|54		1|47							2|21	
Watford (Junction for St. Albans)	"	12|47				1|33							1|55		2| 6							2|39	
King's Langley & Abbot's Langley	"	12|52			1|19	1|38							2| 0		2|12							2|44	
Apsley	"	12|57				1|43							2| 5		2|15							2|49	
Hemel Hempsted & Boxmoor★	"	1| 4			1|27	1|48	1|48						2| 9		2|19							2|54	
Berkhamsted	"	1|12			1|34	1|54	1|56						2|16		2|27							3| 3	
Tring★	"	1|19			1|41	2| 3							2|23		2|34							3|10	
Cheddington	"	1|27			1|48										2|41							3|21	
Leighton Buzzard (Junction for Luton)	"	1|35			1|55										2|44							3|31	
Bletchley	arr.	1|43			2| 5										3| 1							3|41	
Cambridge	dep.	Stop														3	11						Stop	
Oxford																							
Banbury (Merton Street)	arr.																						
Bletchley	dep.	1|20		1|55																			
Wolverton (for Stony Stratford)	"	1|30		2| 4																			
Castlethorpe	"	1|35		2| 9																			
Roade	"	1|44		2|18																			
Blisworth	arr.	1	50																					
Northampton (Castle)	arr.	2| 8		2|29																			
	dep.	1|38		2|40	Stop																		
Blisworth	dep.	1	52																					
Weedon (Junction for Daventry)	"	2	2																					
Welton	"	2	10																					
Rugby	arr.	2|22		3|12					2|57			2|57											
Leamington Spa	arr.	3| 4		Stop																			4|25
Rugby	dep. for Birmingham																						
Coventry	arr.																						
Birmingham (New Street)	"											3	50										3	57
Walsall	"											3	58										4	28
Dudley	"											4	49										5dp 0
Wolverhampton	"																						4	51
Leamington Spa	dep.		1R34	na50										1	50								4	53
Coventry	"		12R57	na15										2	46								Stop
Rugby	dep. for North		2	21	2	21					2R14		2R14	2R14										
Brinklow	"		2|30						3| 0		3| 0	3| 0										
Shilton	"		2	36																				
Nuneaton (Trent Valley)	arr.		2|46	2|46																			
Leicester	dep. for North																						
Nuneaton (Trent Valley)	dep.			2	55										Stop							2n16	2n16
Atherstone	"			3	3																	4	5	4	5
Polesworth	"			3	10																	4	13	4	13
Tamworth (Low Level)	"			3	18																	4	21	4	21
Lichfield (Trent Valley)	arr./dep.												3	35 / 3	45									Stop
Armitage	"												3bf57									
Rugeley (Trent Valley)	"												4bf4									
Colwich	"												4	11									
Milford & Brocton (for Cannock Chase)	"												4	17									
Stafford	arr. from Rugby												4	22 / 4	30									
Birmingham (New Street)	dep.												3	45									
Walsall	"												3	44									
Dudley	"												3	42									
Wolverhampton	"												4	13									
Stafford	arr. from Birmingham												4	31									
Shrewsbury	arr.								5C53		5S53		6	23									
Stafford	dep.											3	40	4	34									
Great Bridgeford	"												4	37									
Norton Bridge	"											3	48	4	43									
Stoke-on-Trent	arr.		3	21										4	47									
Macclesfield (Hibel Road)	"		5	12		5ST48								5	18									
Standon Bridge	dep.											4	12	6	13									
Whitmore	"											5	12										
Madeley	"																					
Betley Road	"																					
CREWE	arr. from South								4	26		4	25		5	7									
Crewe	dep. for Manchester												5	7									
Stockport	arr.		4|14		4| 7 / 4|24 / 5| 6							5|13									6|31
Manchester (Victoria / London Road)	"		4|32		5|25							5|37 / 5|47									7| 2 / 6|45
Bolton (Trinity Street)	"		5	33		5	39				6A11			5	53 / 6	3									7	29
Blackburn	"		6au37		6	42				6P41		6P42	6§49 / 7§15	6A20								8V 0
Burnley (Bank Top)	"		6au15		7	26				7P26		7P26	7§21 / 6W50									8§42
Colne	"		6au28		7§19				7P41		7P41	7§58 / 7W36									8§59
Oldham (Clegg Street)	"		5au07		6au34							8§14 / 7W41									7	21
Rochdale	"		5§29		6§21							7A24 / 6TA84									7	49
Huddersfield	"		5	40		6ts10							7§13 / 7§13									8	44
Halifax	"		6§16		6ts 8							7	16 / 7	21									8V39
Bradford (Exchange)	"		6§40		6ts17							8	3 / 8	3									9V 6
Crewe	dep. for Liverpool											8	32 / 8	32									
Liverpool (Lime Street)	arr.				4|20 / 5|21				5| 5 / 6|17		5| 5 / 6|17										
Crewe	dep. for Holyhead																					
Chester	arr.								4	53		4	53		5	10									
Birkenhead (Woodside)	"								5	0		5	0		5KA40									
Rhyl	"								6	2		5	2		6SX16									
Colwyn Bay	"								5	43		5	43		6SX40									
Llandudno	"								6	6		6	6		7SX 5									
Bangor	"								6	32		6	32		7SX24									
Holyhead	"								6	46		6	46											
Kingstown Pier (Dun Laoghaire)	"								7	55		7	55											
Dublin (Westland Row)	"																					
Crewe	dep. for North																					
Warrington (Bank Quay)	"				4	17				4	27		4	26		4	40	4	52							
Wigan (North Western)	arr.								4	53				5	53									
Southport (Chapel Street)	"								5	27				5	53									
Preston	arr.								6A58				6	A1									
Blackpool (North / Central)	arr.				5	24				5	29		5	24											
Fleetwood	"								6	51		6	51		7	3									
Lancaster (Castle)	"				6	12				6	36		6	30											
Morecambe (Euston Road)	arr.				6|30				6|30		6|30		7|15									
Heysham	"												6	45	6	30								
Belfast	"												7	8	7	8								
Windermere	arr.																					
Penrith (for Ullswater Lake)	arr.								6|57		7| 9		7|20	7|13								
Keswick	"										7	3		7	53	7	15								
Carlisle	arr.												8	50	8	50								
Edinburgh (Princes Street)	arr.				6|13	6|50			7|24		7|24		7|44 / 7|44	9|55							
Glasgow (Central)	"												9	45	9	55								
Perth	"				8	0	9	5			9	56				9	56	6	9							
Dundee (West)	"													11	28								
Aberdeen	"								10	41													
Inverness	"								5	0 / 5	45				5	0									

For connectional trains from Euston, Broad Street, and intermediate Stations to Watford Junction, see London Suburban Official Time Table.

For Notes see page 80.

71

Right from the early days the section over Shap between Carnforth and Carlisle regularly produced double heading; today it is rare but not unknown. *Top left* is an up Anglo-Scottish express for London leaving Carlisle behind a Jumbo 2–4–0 and an Experiment 4–6–0 in the first decade of the present century. *Bottom left:* A pair of Claughton 4–6–0s, No 2416 piloting No 1407, with a Glasgow–Euston express accelerate out of Carlisle with the leading engine seemingly doing all the work; the date is 1924. *Above:* A pair of Class 87 electric locomotives, Nos 87007 and 87026, head the combined 09.43 Liverpool and 09.50 from Manchester to Glasgow on 20 May 1974.

L&GRP (2); G T Heavyside

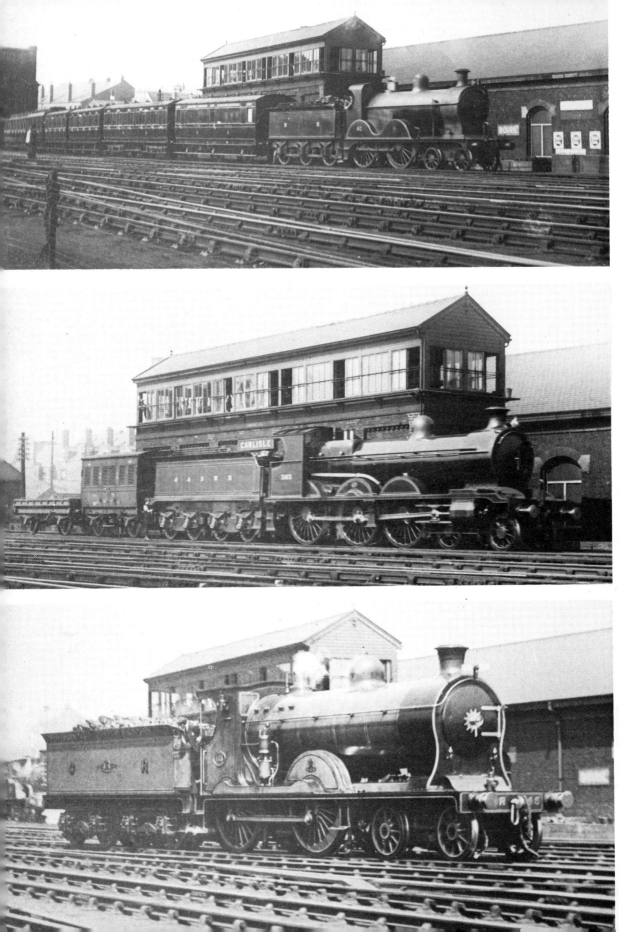

Carlisle in pre-grouping days before 1923 was not only one of the most colourful stations with so much variety in liveries of the different railways using the station, but it really was the frontier station between England and Scotland, and for in normal circumstances locomotives belonging to the English companies never worked north of Carlisle and conversely Scottish-based locomotives never worked south of the station. Indeed right at the start of railways between England and Scotland, as John Thomas points out in his book *The Scottish Railway*, the last remnant of customs formalities was carried out there for although, following the Act of Union, Scotland and England were one for customs purposes, even in the mid 1800s duty was still levied on Scotch whisky coming into England. If Scottish moves for independence succeed history might repeat itself! *Top left:* Midland No 82, one of Johnson's 4–4–0s, much rebuilt by Deeley, leaves Carlisle with a semi-fast train for Leeds and is about to do battle with the Midland route through the Pennines over Blea Moor. *Centre left:* One of the Glasgow & South Western Railway Manson 4–6–0s, No 383, built in 1903 and used on the principal expresses between Carlisle and Glasgow via the GSW line through Kilmarnock, the route used by the Midland Railway's Anglo-Scottish services. *Bottom left:* Caledonian McIntosh 140 Class 4–4–0 No 145 built in 1905 and allocated to Carlisle for workings to Glasgow and Edinburgh.

L&GRP

Above: Carlisle saw the working by the last official BR steam train at the end of steam in 1968. Britannia Pacific No 70013 *Oliver Cromwell* comes to a stand at Carlisle on the run from Liverpool and Manchester on 11 August 1968.

I S Carr

Caledonian 4–4–0 No 733, one of the celebrated Dunalastair I class locomotives, built in 1896, passes Caldew
Junction about one mile north of Carlisle with a northbound Anglo-Scottish express. Following the races to the
north in 1888 and 1895, timings of West Coast expresses
had been considerably tightened up and these engines
were often called upon to perform throughout average
speeds of 50mph or more between Carlisle and Glasgow
or Edinburgh, notwithstanding the climb to Beattock
summit. Notice the semaphore route indicator which with
the arms of the semaphore indicator set at different angles
the Caledonian used to denote the route by which the train
was travelling.

L&GRP

A little further north was Etterby Junction where the railway crossed the River Eden; it also marked the southern
boundary of what later became the extensive Carlisle marshalling yard and the locomotive depot at Kingmoor. A
Dunalastair II 4–4–0 No 771 coasts past Etterby Junction with a southbound West Coast train around the turn
of the century.

L&GRP

Another view of Etterby Junction, this time on 17 June
1961 showing the expansion which has taken place in the
intervening years. Additional tracks were provided from
here to Caldew Junction during the second world war and
the new brick-built signalbox constructed a few yards
north of the original. Even that has now gone as part of the
electrification and resignalling of the entire West Coast
main line. Britannia Pacific No 70015 *Apollo* approaches
the same set of points depicted in the bottom left photograph with a Glasgow–Manchester express.

Kenneth Field

Above: English Electric Class 40 diesel No D322 heads north past Quintinshill signalbox with the northbound Royal Scot from Euston to Glasgow on 9 September 1961. It is a little difficult to imagine the scene 46 years earlier on the morning of 22 May 1915 when three passenger trains were involved in a massive double collision also involving two freight trains standing on the goods loops on each side, the worst accident ever in British railway history with 227 passengers killed and 246 injured, most of them men of the Seventh Batallion of the Royal Scots on their way to serve in the first world war.

Derek Cross

Below: Bustling Beattock in the heyday of steam, with Class 5 4–6–0 No 45236 passing at the head of a Crewe-Perth express while 2–8–0 No 48612 and Class 5 4–6–0 No 44955 wait in the yard with freights for a path northwards over Beattock summit.

Derek Cross

The 10 miles of steep climbing from Beattock station to Beattock summit, mostly at 1 in 74, is one of the most testing stretches of any British main line, rising to a summit of just over 1,000ft. *Top:* An English Electric Class 50 diesel climbs steadily towards Beattock summit with a Euston–Glasgow express and crosses the dual carriageway A74 trunk road on 30 August 1973.

G T Heavyside

Nearly all freight trains and many passenger trains in steam days needed assistance over Beattock; Fairburn Class 4 2–6–4T No 42693 steadily banks a heavy freight towards Greskine, halfway up the climb, on 15 August 1964.

John Goss

Stanier Class 5 4–6–0 No 44793 drifts down the southern side of Beattock bank with a southbound freight on 23 May 1963. The A74 trunk road between Carlisle and Glasgow at this stage looks but little more than a country lane although road works on the lefthand side are in progress to enlarge it to a dual carriageway.

Derek Cross

Below: W H Auden's poem *Night Mail*, portraying the West Coast postal as it pounds up the long climb to Beattock summit in steam days and used in the film of that name made by the Post Office in the 1930s. The rhythm of the first two verses matches the slow measured coach wheelbeats on the climb, but the pace quickens in verse four as the train speeds up.

NIGHT MAIL

This is the night mail crossing the border,
Bringing the cheque and the postal order,
Letters for the rich, letters for the poor,
The shop at the corner and the girl next door,
Pulling up Beattock, a steady climb –
The gradient's against her but she's on time.

Past cotton grass and moorland boulder,
Shovelling white steam over her shoulder,
Snorting noisily as she passes
Silent miles of wind-swept grasses;
Birds turn their heads as she approaches,
Stare from the bushes at her blank-faced coaches;
Sheep dogs cannot turn her course,
They slumber on with paws across,
In the farm she passes no one wakes,
But a jug in the bedroom gently shakes.

Dawn freshens, the climb is done,
Down towards Glasgow she descends
Towards the steam tugs, yelping down the glade of cranes
Towards the fields of apparatus, the furnaces
Set on the dark plain like gigantic chessmen.
All Scotland waits for her;
In the dark glens, beside the pale-green sea lochs,
Men long for news.

Letters of thanks, letters from banks,
Letters of joy from the girl and boy,
Receipted bills and invitations
To inspect new stock or visit relations,
And applications for situations,
And timid lovers' declarations,
And gossip, gossip from all the nations,
News circumstantial, news financial,
Letters with holiday snaps to enlarge in
Letters with faces scrawled on the margin.

Letters from uncles, cousins and aunts,
Letters to Scotland from the South of France,
Letters of condolence to Highlands and Lowlands,
Notes from overseas to the Hebrides;
Written on paper of every hue,
The pink, the violet, the white and the blue;
The chatty, the catty, the boring, adoring,
The cold and official and the heart's outpouring,
Clever, stupid, short and long,
The typed and the printed and the spelt all wrong.

Thousands are still asleep
Dreaming of terrifying monsters
Or a friendly tea beside the band at Cranston's or Crawford's;
Asleep in working Glasgow, asleep in well-set Edinburgh,
Asleep in Granite Aberdeen.
They continue their dreams
But shall wake soon and long for letters.
And none will hear the postman's knock
Without a quickening of the heart,
For who can bear to feel himself forgotten?

W. H. AUDEN.

Soon after the inauguration of electrification through to Glasgow on the West Coast main line a Class 86 electric locomotive climbs the northern approach to Beattock with the 11.45 Euston–Glasgow on 20 May 1974. The burn in the foreground is one of the tributary streams of the River Anan whose valley with that of the Clyde was adopted after much wrangling by the railway builders of the 1840s.

G T Heavyside

The LMS Royal Scot 4–6–0s introduced in 1927 transformed the principal express services on the West Coast main line. Despite the speed at which they were designed and built, they were really remarkable engines, capable of hard running with heavy loads single handed. The first batch of 50 engines was built by the North British Locomotive Company at its two works in Glasgow and as engines were commissioned they were quickly put to work on the heaviest Anglo-Scottish trains. Here No 6128 then named *Meteor* heads the Royal Scot train through Lanarkshire soon after it was placed in service in 1927. Notice the continued use of the Caledonian semaphore route indicator at the top of the smokebox door.

Mitchell Library, courtesy John Thomas

Table 65 — Mondays to Saturdays

London to Glasgow

	A	B SO	C ①		D FO		A	E SO		A	G SO	①
London Euston .. — — 59, 66 d	12 50	12 55	..		13 00	..	13 45	13 50	..	13 55	..	14 00
Watford Junction .... 59, 66 d	..	..	..		12 24							13 24
Bletchley .. .. .. 66 d	..	..	..		12 58							13 58
66 Northampton .... 66 d					13 22							14 22
Rugby .. .. .. 66 d					14 01							14 59
18 Leicester........................ d												14 37
Nuneaton .. .. .. d											15 13	15 23
Atherstone........................ d												15 29
Polesworth .. .. .. d												15 35
Tamworth .. .. .. d												15 40
Lichfield Trent Valley .. .. d												15 49
Rugeley .. .. .. d												15 58
66 Coventry .. .. .. d							13 48	14 18				
69 Birmingham New Street........ d			14 05		14 13		14 38	14 55				
69 Wolverhampton .. .. d			14 24		14 42		15 05	15 12				
Stafford........................ 69 d		14 34			14 42	15 01	15 25	15 30				16 09
69 Stoke-on-Trent .. .. a							16 17	15 44				
69 Macclesfield .... a							16 45	16 06				
Crewe .. .. a	14 54	14 59	15 03	15 10	15 29		15 50	15 54				16 07
81 Wilmslow .. .. .. a		15s15	15s26	15 52								16 52
81 Stockport .. .. .. a		15s25	15s37	16 03				16s23				17 03
81 Manchester Piccadilly........ a		15 34	15s46	16 14				16 32				17 14
82 Runcorn .. .. .. a	15s06			15 47	15s54	16s06	16 19	16 21				16 42
82 Liverpool Lime Street.......... a	15 27			16 13	16s16	16 27	16 36	16 43				17 08
83 Holyhead .. .. .. a				17 57								
Crewe .. .. .. d			15 06									16 12
Warrington Bank Quay.. .. d												16 31
99 Liverpool Lime Street.......... d												15s38
Wigan North Western .. .. d												16 43
Preston .. .. .. a			15 43		16 20							16 56
96 Blackpool North .. .. a			16 35		17c07							17 41
96 Manchester Victoria............ d			14b15	15 15								
96 Bolton.......................... d			14b32	15 32								
96 Blackpool North.................. d			14 45	15 45								
Preston .. .. .. 109 d			15 45	16 22								
Lancaster...................... 109 d			16 05	17a04						17 15	17a49	
109 Heysham .. .. .. a												
109 Barrow-in-Furness .. .. a			17 16	18 11							18 55	
Oxenholme .. .. .. d										17 40		
110 Windermere .... a										18 05		
Penrith .. .. .. d												
Carlisle .. .. .. d			17 00		17 31							
.. .. .. d			17 03		17 33							
Annan.......................... a												
Dumfries .. .. .. a										17 28		
Kirkconnel........................ a												
Kilmarnock .. .. 222 a										18 43		
Lockerbie .. .. .. a					17 54							
Carstairs .. — — 224 a			17 56									
224 d			18 01	18 03								
Haymarket .. 225, 228, 241 a			18 38									
Edinburgh .. 225, 228, 241 a			18 42									
Motherwell .. .. 224 a			18s19									
Glasgow Central........ 222, 224 a			18 35				18 57			19 35		
Coatbridge Central .. .. 229 a												
Larbert .. .. .. 229 a			19p35		20p18					21p35		
Stirling .. .. .. 229 a			19p46		20p28					21p46		
Perth.......................... 229 a			20p30		21p12					22p30		
Aviemore........................ 229 a			22v45									
Inverness...................... 229 a												

For general notes see pages 2-4

For complete service between London and Birmingham see Table 66, Birmingham and Manchester see Table 69, Preston and Lancaster see Table 109

A ✗ and ⊡ Mondays to Fridays. ⊡ Saturdays
B 21 June to 13 September
C ① to Glasgow
D 30 May to 3 October
E 14 June to 13 September
G 14 June to 30 August

b Saturdays until 25 October Manchester Victoria dep. 14 45, Bolton dep. 15 02
c Mondays to Fridays. Saturdays until 25 October arr. 17 06
e Liverpool Exchange. Change at Ormskirk and Preston (Table 100)
p Via Glasgow Central and Glasgow Queen Street. Passengers make their own way from one station to the other
v Fridays only 7 November to 2 April. Via Glasgow Central and Glasgow Queen Street. Passengers make their own way from one station to the other.

Culmination of British Railways modernisation of the West Coast route was electrification in 1974. This page from the 1975 timetable demonstrates the striking advance in speed by comparison with previous timetable extracts illustrated in this book. The 13.45 from Euston is due at Glasgow at 18.57 in 5hr 12min including three intermediate stops, compared with the Coronation Scot's 6hr 30min with one stop.

Caledonian Pickersgill 4–4–0 No 14492 formerly Caledonian No 87 built in 1921 approaches Beattock summit with a southbound express in 1926.

L&GRP

Below: A little further to the north an example of one of the Caledonian freight classes to survive well into British Railways days, the Class 812 0–6–0 designed by McIntosh just before the turn of the century for mixed traffic duties, here seen as BR No 57568, climbs towards Beattock summit with a southbound ballast and engineers train in July 1962. One of these locomotives has been preserved in Glasgow Transport Museum.

Derek Cross

Occasionally when the East Coast main line is blocked for any reason between Edinburgh and Newcastle, East Coast route expresses are diverted over the West Coast route, via Carstairs and Carlisle, regaining their normal route by the cross-country line from Carlisle to Newcastle. Deltic Class 55 diesel locomotive No D9017 heads an Edinburgh–Kings Cross express on the east to south spur of the triangle at Carstairs, and gains the West Coast main line at Strawfrank Junction on 23 July 1972.

Derek Cross

Towards the end of steam working at the north end of the West Coast main line in Scotland former LNER Pacifics appeared on a number of services between Perth, and Carstairs or Carlisle. The Aberdeen portion of the up West Coast postal arrives at Motherwell behind Class A2/3 4–6–2 No 60524 *Herringbone* which it will take through to Carstairs for remarshalling with the Glasgow portion for the onward journey to London. This photograph was taken on 24 June 1963.

M Bryce

What a delightful engine to have as station pilot in 1906 at Glasgow Central! This was a Conner goods engine originally built in 1868 and later rebuilt by Drummond for passenger service but by the turn of the century displaced on these duties by more modern 4–4–0s.

L&GRP

A Glasgow Central–Gourock suburban train in the first decade of the present century headed by one of McIntosh's 4–6–0s, No 916 of the 908 class. These engines were basically designed for express goods work but a number were employed on the principal Gourock line boat trains from Glasgow which were in competition with similar services of the North British and Glasgow & South Western railways. The coaches used on these services in Caledonian days were among the best in the country on this sort of work.

L&GRP

End of the journey for a West Coast route express from Euston as it approaches Glasgow Central over the Clyde bridge behind Class 50s Nos 422 and 401 on 9 May 1972. Although the West Coast route to Glasgow was completed in 1849 today's route into Glasgow from Motherwell, crossing the Clyde at the approaches to Glasgow Central, was not completed until 1879.

G T Heavyside

An up West Coast route express leaves Glasgow Central for Manchester on the evening of 23 May 1974 headed by electric locomotive No 87011, which is seen here easing out on to the Clyde bridge.

G T Heavyside

Chronology

Opening dates

Euston–Boxmoor (first section of London & Birmingham Railway)	20 July 1837
Completion of London & Birmingham Railway	17 September 1838
Rugby–Stafford (Trent Valley Railway)	26 June 1847
Birmingham–Stafford–Warrington (Grand Junction Railway)	4 July 1837
Parkside–Wigan (North Union)	July 1832
Wigan–Preston (North Union)	1838
(North Union later jointly owned by LNWR and L&YR)	
Preston–Lancaster	26 June 1840
Lancaster–Carlisle throughout	17 December 1846
Carlisle–Glasgow Townend throughout (Caledonian Railway)	15 February 1848
(the latter section completed the West Coast route between London and Glasgow)	
Glasgow Central station as principal terminus for the south	1879
Amalgamation of London & Birmingham, Trent Valley Railway, and Grand Junction Railway to form London & North Western Railway (Lancaster & Carlisle absorbed by LNWR in 1879)	18 July 1846
Railway grouping – London & North Western and Caledonian railways become part of the London Midland & Scottish Railway	1 January 1923
Nationalisation of group companies. LMS forms London Midland Region and part of Scottish Region	1 January 1948
First diesel working by LMS main-line diesel locomotives on West Coast route	4 October 1948
General introduction of BR Type 40 diesels to West Coast route	1959/60
Gradual run-down of steam locomotives on West Coast express duties	1963/4
Surviving LMS express steam locomotives banned south of Crewe because of insufficient clearance under electrification catenary	1 September 1964
Last regular steam workings in Lancashire and on BR	4 August 1968
Electrification of main line at 25,000 volts ac	
Inaugural section Manchester–Crewe	12 September 1960
Completion Euston–Liverpool/Manchester (Full electric timetable)	18 April 1966
Completion of Birmingham area (Full timetable)	6 March 1967
Completion Crewe–Glasgow (Full timetable)	6 May 1974

Comparative times, Euston-Glasgow

Date	1887	1910	1938	1976
Train from Euston	10.00	10.00	13.30†	10.45
Overall time	9hr 45min	8hr 15min	6hr 30min	5hr
No of stops	7*	5	1	1

* Including 25min stop at Preston for Lunch
† The Coronation Scot

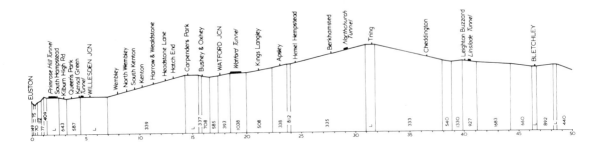

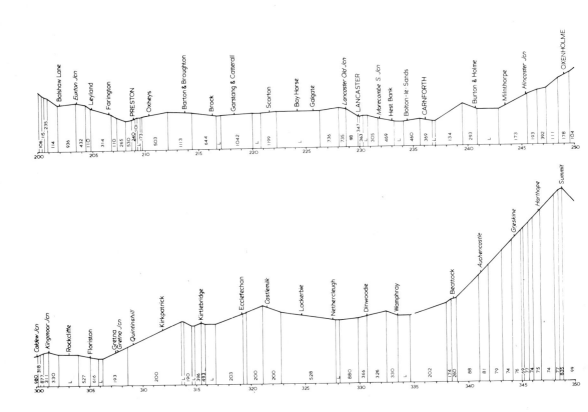

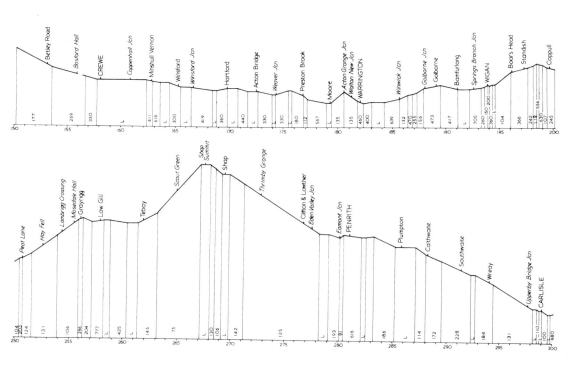

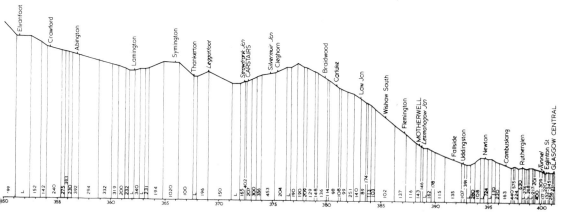

Further reading

about the West Coast route and the areas through which it passes

Ashmore, Owen. *Industrial Archaeology of Lancashire* (David & Charles, 1969)
Biddle, Gordon. *Victorian Stations* (David & Charles, 1973)
Butt, John. *Industrial Archaeology of Scotland* (David & Charles, 1967)
Christiansen, Rex. *A Regional History of the Railways of Great Britain. Vol 7 The West Midlands* (David & Charles, 1973)
Cornwell, H J C. *Forty Years of Caledonian Locomotives 1882–1922* (David & Charles, 1974)
Donaghy, Thomas J. *Liverpool & Manchester Railway Operations 1831–1845* (David & Charles, 1972)
Ellis, C Hamilton. *British Railway History* in two vols (George Allen & Unwin, 1954)
Hadfield, Charles. *The Canals of the East Midlands* (David & Charles, 1970)
——and Biddle, Gordon. *The Canals of North West England* in two vols (David & Charles, 1970)
Hardy, Eric. *The Naturalist in Lakeland* (David & Charles, 1973)
Kichenside, G M and Williams, A R: *British Railway Signalling* 3rd Edition (Ian Allan, 1975)
Knowlton, Derrick. *The Naturalist in Scotland* (David & Charles, 1974)
Marshall, J D. *Old Lakeland* (David & Charles, 1971)
——and Davies-Shiel, M. *The Lake District at Work* (David & Charles, 1971)
Nock, O S. *The Caledonian Dunalastairs* (David & Charles, 1968)
—— *Electric Euston to Glasgow* (Ian Allan, 1974)
—— *The LNWR Precursor Family* (David & Charles, 1966)
—— *North Western* (Ian Allan, 1968)
—— *The Railway Race to the North* (Ian Allan, 1960)
—— *Speed Records on Britain's Railways* (David & Charles, 1971)
Reed, Brian. *150 Years of British Steam Locomotives* (David & Charles, 1975)
Smith, David M. *Industrial Britain, The North West* (David & Charles, 1969)
Smithson, Alison and Peter. *The Euston Arch* (Thames & Hudson, 1968)
Webb, Brian. *English Electric Main Line Diesels of BR* (David & Charles, 1976)
White, H P. *A Regional History of the Railways of Great Britain. Vol 3 Greater London* (David & Charles, 1971)

Bradshaw's April 1910 Railway Guide (Reprinted David & Charles, 1968)
Bradshaw's July 1938 Railway Guide (Reprinted David & Charles, 1969)

Acknowledgements

I should like to thank all the photographers who have supplied photographs from which this book has been compiled, and who have been credited individually, and I must acknowledge the permission of the Post Office for allowing reproduction of W H. Auden's words in *Night Mail*. Finally I must thank John Thomas and Derek Cross for steering me through the historical complications at the northern end of this potential 'international' main line.